Familiar Rivers

David Watts

Copyright © 2024 by David Watts

This is a work of fiction. Names, characters, places, and
incidents either are the product of the author's imagination or
are used
fictitiously. Any resemblance to actual persons, living or dead,
events, or locales is entirely coincidental.

Nicholas David Publications
San Francisco, London

Cover art...........................Gabriel Baranow-Watts
Cover design......................................Kevin Diamond
Book Design.....................................Lauren Gonzalez

FIRST EDITION

Be in harmony with the spring clouds

—Hafiz

Familiar Rivers

David Watts

the designer of the universe is waiting
to see where all this is going

the genome is the universe's way of
making beneficial mistakes

the sex tangle goes a lot deeper
than roughed up genitals

the body is home to its own cosmos

dreams are practice leaving the body

once a month tether moon energy

a touch in the night threads the
darkness

the day your mother-in-law visits
the refrigerator will fill with leftovers

do joy in spite of whatever

two bodies of knowledge,
one handed down,
one acquired by trials and train wrecks

blackstrap molasses is an ambivalent sweetness

things take longer than they take

the scent remains after the rose is gone

melted ice cream tastes better

odd numbers are more interesting

people have that annoying habit
of remembering what you say

if a conversation is agreeable

you won't learn much

if you worry about yourself

your self will start worrying

life gets a little better
when you make fun of it

run a detour through an isolated road

and people will sit on their porches to
watch

if you want to bring rain, pitch a tent

the Post Office at its busiest moment
will have one Window Clerk

for intelligence to be smart
you have to add judgment

at some point we must get out of the
way of our children

half of looking smart is not saying much

in bed on your wedding night,
if a scorpion stings your ear . . .

it might be a bad sign

put your demons to work on something

kindness spreads like springtime

a blessing given is twice received

put enough knowledge together in one
place and things start connecting

to believe your eyes
your heart has to be awake

if humiliation subdues your passion
what will your passion think of you?

put your fear of flying in a box

and leave it on the ground

when you mistake your incoherent
mumblings for philosophy

it's the wine talking

if you don't like this apple
wait a year and they'll make another

with all this research going on
eventually they'll discover that food
is good for you

the world is a cathedral

snowy mountains, the fragrant rose,
the wandering river, as if the spiritual
just keeps showing up in this world

when a product is really good
they'll improve it till it isn't

progress can go a bit too far

being afraid of symptoms
makes two things worse

can't prevent grief from entering

but you can give it an exit plan

some people are so confident in their
ignorance you'd have trouble not
believing them

if you tell a falsehood
someone, somewhere will repeat it
as truth

if we listen to spun news
we become dung worshipers

comedians give the most balanced
newscast because it includes judgment

think slow before acting fast

don't let the past think we weren't
there

as you get older your morning stretch
consists of putting on your socks

there will be those days
when you're the one in the prayer circle
with shit on your shoes

the supernatural might be natural

the object of war is never peace

the soil below our feet contains bits of
consciousness reconnecting

it's hardest to make friends when you most need them

big accomplishments are baskets full of small accomplishments false modesty does not become you

madness is a language with a different
take on words

there's a reason
why some shoes cost less

some Christian conservatives are
neither

read authors who struggle to make a
hard truth simple

more gets taught
in shorter school weeks

memories get whitewashed every few
years

a great fright is to realize that people
you played Little League with are
running big corporations

some parents believe sex education
will be taken care of by the cosmos

pleasure passed around gets larger

pause to check how deep the moment is

there is a quality of understanding that
has nothing to do with intelligence

there's a reasonable chance that the
only thing that lasts after we're gone is
the rumors we've stirred up

always something of value
behind a good temptation

if you imagine something deeply
you will believe it happened

shifty politicians don't want an
educated electorate

there is no human trait more prevalent
in Washington than hypocrisy

come on, even tree roots cooperate

tune in, someone might call your name

every molecule is alive

spare time is imagination food

the biggest fault our faults have is their
refusal to be recognized

if you don't believe in religion
you might be afraid it's true

actions seldom know their aftershocks

seek what is found in the folds of silence

to receive the miraculous
you have to build a landing pad

the only way to find out
what's on the other side of
transformation is to go there

faith is a sensible guess

pick your passions better than you do
your breakfast cereal

you have to believe in hope to have it

freedom enlarges with use

mountains have false summits

a balanced life requires a little
unrestrained joy

chastity is the ruin of the celibate

jealousy chooses justification over truth

why be jealous of your lover's past since
that's what has made the person you
fell in love with

the broken hammer contrives to make
us stop working

if you want to live longer get a
companion

those with the most guns believe they
have permission to use them

the problem with arguments is that you
end up believing what you just said

the secret lover is admired by nature,

trashed by society

curiosity is the afterburner of desire

take away consequence and we become
animals

men are attracted to features in a
woman that suggest she is fertile;

they want their genome to make it into
the next generation

women are attracted to features in a
man that suggest he is successful;

they want their egg to have a good life

the ability to complement someone
shows you are comfortable with
yourself

some are courageous only because they
fear the shame of cowardice

ever wonder how politicians who
legislate budget cuts for children and
the poor retire as millionaires?

it's alright to have no opinion about
stuff

kindness is a friendly boomerang

a forced opinion is anal gas

the study of logic makes sense, turns
out it doesn't much apply to humans

you have to fail penmanship to get into
medical school

I had five mortal illnesses before I could get out of med school

there should be a federal bureau of role
models

the ability to grasp both sides of a
paradox is a path to wisdom

a roomy intelligence delights in
differences

not every message the mouth speaks is
audible

silhouettes are backlit identities

religious fervor easily turns into
unsaintly deeds

think ruthless, practice kindness

a locked door has a knocker on it

keep your antennae in the up position

spring arrives aroma by aroma

no distress so corrosive as a long legal
battle

tears tunnel the interior

words are free and sometimes
expensive

words are collections of echoes

people who hold back something
are interesting

the more complicated an individual the
more likely there will come a
characteristic no one could have
predicted

a poem can topple a crown

just before sleep you are alone
with your deeds of the day

love will mess you up

best not to question how love arrives

putting a name on something gives you
power over it

ghosts shrivel on exposure to light

old age should be populated with as
much childhood as possible

the downward heft of pressure makes a
diamond and a saint

wisdom is a painting made of
knowledge

you don't want to live to a 100?

I'll ask you again when you're 99

your home town knows you too well to
believe your success

the best quality is to be grateful

keep a lookout for your angel

every dawn is a call to beauty

shower your body with self-blessing

inside the aroma of sunshine on soil
there will be butterflies

late at night you can hear the earth sing

may awe arrive in time

With Inspiration From:

Galway Kinnell, Robin Baker,
Gabriel Baranow-Watts, Fritjof Kapra,
Terrence Des Pres, Joan Baranow

145

Made in the USA
Las Vegas, NV
14 December 2024

13967135R00085